★ THE ★
SOUTHERNER'S
INSTRUCTION BOOK

★ THE ★
SOUTHERNER'S
INSTRUCTION BOOK

JIM and SUSAN ERSKINE

PELICAN PUBLISHING COMPANY
Gretna 1995

First printing, March 1994
Second printing, July 1994
Third printing, September 1995

Library of Congress Cataloging-in-Publication Data

Erskine, Jim.
   The southerner's instruction book / by Jim and Susan Erskine ;
illustrated by Jim Erskine.
    p. cm.
   ISBN 1-56554-042-5
   1. Southern States—Humor. I. Erskine, Susan. II. Title.
PN6231.S64E77 1994
818'.5402—dc20

93-43089
CIP

Manufactured in the United States of America
Published by Pelican Publishing Company, Inc.
1101 Monroe Street, Gretna, Louisiana 70053

To our ma's and pa's,
for bringing us up right

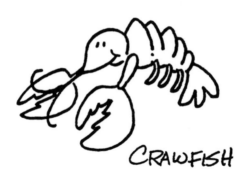

CRAWFISH

Do not talk fast.

~~~

Do not drive slow.

~~~

Always wonder what your daddy would think.

~~~

Always clean your plate.

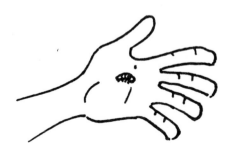

Don't be afraid
to hold
a roly-poly.

Wave to the person in the oncoming car.

Know what chitlins are.

~~~

Know when to say "ma'am" and "sir."

Appreciate moon pies.

Nip it in the bud.

~~~

Know someone named "Bubba."

~~~

Call your sister "sister."

Do not use silverware with fried chicken, corn on the cob, ribs, or watermelon.

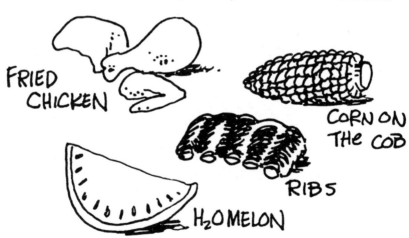

FRIED CHICKEN

CORN ON THE COB

RIBS

H₂O MELON

SILVERWARE A MUST:

CHICKEN FRIED STEAK AND MASHED POTATOES

CHESS PIE

GRITS

PINTO BEANS, CORNBREAD AND SWEET VIDALIA ONIONS

Eat beanie-weenie straight out of the can.

~~~

Have at least one pickup truck
in the immediate family.

Remember that men sweat, women glow.

Never bend over without
hiking up your pants first.

Learn to say "y'all" without
feeling self-conscious.

Good food takes a while to fix.

~~~

Always say the blessing before you begin the meal.

~~~

Keep your elbows off the table.

A good biscuit
will almost always
make up for a bad meal.

Always refer to ladies as ladies.

Say "please" without fail.

~~~

Take home a plate
to whoever missed the pot luck.

~~~

Take along the bug spray.

Never drink the last diet Coke.

Don't ever pay
for a "gimme" cap.

MOSQUITO:
OFFICIAL BIRD of the SOUTH

Learn to thump your watermelons.

At least try the pecan pie.

Every May, expect to see
at least one teen-aged girl
wearing a prom dress
pumping gas at the
convenience store.

Remember Jesus loves you.

Behave yourself.

~~~

If your time ain't come,
not even a doctor can kill you.

Squirt some chocolate syrup in your Coke.

It's okay to cuss fire ants.

~~~

Learn how to shell beans.

~~~

Be baptized in a creek.

~~~

Take in strays.

Don't avoid the family reunion
(unless you want this decision to be the topic
of all future family conversations).

  Learn to milk
your own cow.

Iced tea tastes best
when you're in your bathrobe.

Stop and smell the honeysuckle.

~~~

Let the kids camp out in the backyard.

Learn to tell a really scary ghost story.

~~~

Schedule your TV viewing
around Andy Griffith reruns.

Attend a revival
at least once a year.

Pay attention to your
grandparents' stories.

Learn to drive a tractor.

Know which BBQ is the best in town.

~~~

If you're not wearing a jacket,
roll up your sleeves.

~~~

Proper women wear red lipstick only at night.

~~~

Know the difference between a second cousin
and a first cousin once removed.

~~~

Put plenty of salt in the ice
when making ice cream.

Don't stop having children
until all the grandparents
have namesakes.

~~~

Take the longest stick you can find
to the weenie roast.

~~~

Never forget the s'mores.

~~~

Flip over june bugs that are stuck on their backs.

~~~

Let folks off the hook without making a scene.

If you invite trouble,
don't fuss if it accepts.

~~~

The only mark some folks ever make in life
is on someone else's fender.

~~~

Flirt with your waitress, but leave a good tip.

~~~

Always drive down a dirt road
fast enough
to keep ahead of your dust.

The best place to be during a thunderstorm
is the front porch swing.

Drink your peanuts in an RC.

Pull over whenever you meet
a funeral procession.

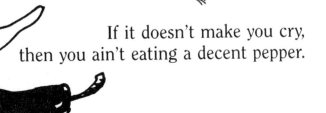

If it doesn't make you cry,
then you ain't eating a decent pepper.

Nothing has more lives than a lie.

~~~

Never look up at a blackbird roost.

~~~

Some possums are just destined to meet
their fate under your car.

HONK
HONK!!

Hell is God giving you just
what you thought you wanted.

The preacher will never
let you out on time.

If he's really wound up,
he may even unplug the clock.

"Just As I Am" always has
more verses than what's
in the hymnal.

Never pass up
a good yard sale.

Strawberries taste best
when you're picking them.

A good cheese ball
is appropriate
for any social gathering.

After a hike,
check yourself for ticks.

Never chase a polecat.

~~~

Krystals should be eaten by the bag.

~~~

A country store is the best place in the world
to purchase a baloney sandwich.

~~~

The best baloney sandwich
is at least one-quarter inch thick
with Miracle Whip on white bread.

~~~

You can always fit into those jeans
one more time.

Let the minnows nibble on your toes.

~~~

The friendly guy who asks you
"How are they bitin'?"
is always the game warden.

~~~

An RC goes with everything.

~~~

Resist all inclinations to enunciate properly.

~~~

BBQ and white shirts do not mix.

Fish often.

Be sociable to your fellow man,
even if you don't particularly like him
or know him from a hole in the ground.

~~~

The three most stubborn things in the world
are a mule, a polecat,
and an angry wife.

~~~

If Mama ain't happy,
ain't nobody happy.

~~~

Do right now so you won't have to make right later.

There's no shame in getting dirty—
only shame in staying dirty.

~~~

The South is the best place
in the world to be an old lady.

If you're too old to be sexy, cause trouble.

The best biscuit is a hot biscuit.

The uglier
the dinner menu,
the better the food.

Memorize the books of the Bible.

~~~

The slower you talk, the better your words taste.

~~~

It's not the heat, it's the humidity.

~~~

See Rock City.

~~~

When life brings you trouble,
turning it into
an adventure
is the best thing you can do.

Don't ever pick a fight
with a man who's chewing tobacco.

~~~

A good laugh is better than a dose of salts.

Grits taste best
with plenty
of red-eye gravy.

Too much of anything ain't healthy.

~~~

Expect a politician's bumper stickers
to last longer than his promises.

There's a little boy inside many stuffed shirts.

~~~

Nobody gets hurt from words you don't say.

~~~

Just because someone hasn't had a chance to steal
don't mean he's honest.

The damn fool
driver is always
the other guy.

If you're going to cuss the other driver,
make sure your windows are rolled up.

A friend is the person
who will tell you you have a piece of food
stuck between your teeth.

~~~

Keep your mouth shut and you won't
stick your foot in it.

~~~

One of the hardest things to put up with
is a good example.

~~~

Sweat has never drowned anybody.

~~~

It's better to grow old than the alternative.

If it's cheap, it's too expensive.

Old dogs are pleasanter
company than some folks.

You can't just
concentrate on one side
of an ice-cream cone.

The home hasn't been built
that can peaceably house
you and your mother-in-law.

The best time to give advice
is before trouble starts.

~~~

Somebody's got to get dirty
if the barn's going to get clean.

~~~

If you've got no choice, be courageous.

~~~

Experience is just another way
to say you screwed up.

~~~

You ain't ever too old
to learn something stupid.

If you talk the talk,
you better walk the walk.

~~~

Borrowing money is just like scratching:
it only feels good for a little while.

The hardest thing to do
is what your neighbors aren't.

Right is right and
wrong is wrong,
no matter how many yahoos
say otherwise.

THE
WISHBONE –
CAUSE OF UNTOLD
FIGHTS BETWEEN
SOUTHERN SIBLINGS.

If you keep getting a "no"
then you ain't asking the question right.

~~~

Strangers are more so
the farther north you go.

~~~

Nobody pees on an electric fence twice.

~~~

If you find you can't make a choice,
then you've made one.

~~~

A Port-a-potty suffers
from being a mite too popular.

Never walk across
a hot parking lot
barefoot.

The sooner you stop and ask directions,
the less you'll have to listen to your wife fuss.

~~~

Don't let the grass
grow under your feet.

~~~

The wise man remembers his wife's birthday
but forgets her age.

~~~

There is a direct correlation
between the humidity
and the cost of your new perm.

If you spit out gossip, it's bound to splat
back in your face.

~~~

Everybody is somebody else's eccentric.

~~~

The best way
to take your mind off your troubles
is to wear shoes two sizes too small.

~~~

It's easier to get into trouble than out of it.

~~~

Don't ever drink more
than you can walk out with.

The length of the line
is in direct proportion
to how bad you have to use the rest room.

~~~

The past always looks better than it was
because it ain't here anymore.

~~~

You know how you really
feel about your neighbor
when a "For Sale" sign
goes up in front of his house.

~~~

Nothing helps you drive better than
a police car behind you.

The first bug to hit your windshield is
bound to land right in front of your eyes.

The softer the bread, the harder the butter.

~~~

You show a lot about yourself by what you laugh at.

~~~

If you can admit you're wrong
when you're wrong, you're all right.

Your kid is that object
that stands halfway
between you and the TV set.

The only stoplight in town
is always red.

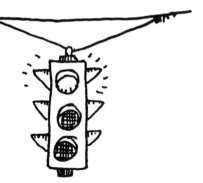

A dog is the only thing in the world that loves you more than you love yourself.

If you're going to spit out the car window, make sure it's open and the back one's closed.

The more cars in the front yard, the less desirable the neighbor.

Any yard worth
its salt will have
at least a few
pink flamingoes in it.

The older the iron skillet,
the tastier the corn bread.

Lazy is leaving your Christmas lights
hanging the whole year.

Be humble.

~~~

Always ask; never tell.

~~~

Don't abide biggety folks.

~~~

Learn to mosey.

~~~

It is possible to elevate piddling to a fine art.

~~~

At a four-way stop,
always defer
to the most dented-up vehicle.

The faster you need to be somewhere,
the more tractors
there will be on the road.

~~~

The more you want to take your time
and enjoy the view,
the larger the semi tailgating you.

~~~

The only time the conversation in the next room pauses
is when you're ready to flush.

~~~

Slugs are for salting.

The best ice cream is ice cream
you've cranked yourself.

~~~

God made armadillos to test
your braking
reflexes.

ARMADILLO
(POSSUM on the HALF-SHELL)

Never let the dog
nuzzle you
after he's been
drinking
from the toilet.

It takes a surefooted dog
to ride on top of a pickup truck.

An hour of whittlin' is worth two of frettin'.

~~~

Sit down a spell, whenever you're invited to.

A front porch swing
is for sparkin', snoozin',
and listenin'
to the neighbors argue.

If you're going to spit,
be sure you hit what you aim at.

~~~

If you work up a sweat whittlin',
then you ain't doin' it right.

~~~

Always say grace before meals.

A gentleman always leaves
the toilet seat down.

~~~

Read your Bible every day.

~~~

It's okay to skip the "begats."

~~~

That BB gun will put your eye out.

~~~

Mobile homes aren't.

~~~

A good garden is a work of art.

The first tomato out of the garden
always tastes best.

~~~

The last tomato out of the garden
is a relief.

~~~

There is never enough sweet corn.

~~~

There is always too much squash.

A pond is to listen to.

Frogs are to gig.

Kudzu is to take your frustrations out on.

~~~

June bugs are
for tying a string to.

Even good friends need to leave sometime.

~~~

You know you're no longer welcome as a guest
when your host suggests everyone
fend for himself at mealtime.

A sprinkler is to run through.

The best way to say goodbye
is to wave a lot, smile big,
and keep moving toward the door.

~~~

Too much hospitality
makes everyone sick of everyone else.

~~~

Dance with who brought you.

~~~

Always offer to bait the lady's hook.

~~~

Resist the urge to correct your grandpa's stories.

Be sure you have on clean underwear, in case you're in an accident.

Stand at the front door and wave until your company has driven out of sight.

A toothpick is required apparel after eating in a restaurant.

Car keys are also for cleaning the wax out of your ears.

Never spit in a lady's wastebasket.

Never spit
in the
collection plate.

Clean your plate because there are people
going hungry in Africa.

~~~

Leave food on your plate if you are female.

~~~

Don't track mud into the house.

When someone says, "Pass me a biscuit,"
pass the entire plate.

~~~

Leave a light on for whoever isn't home yet.

~~~

Yankees don't know any better.

~~~

Stand whenever "Dixie" is played.

~~~

The only time it's okay to fuss about the food
is if you cooked it.

CATFISH

Use it up,
wear it out,
make it do,
or do without.

~~~

A good fence makes a good neighbor.

~~~

If it ain't broke, don't fix it.

~~~

Sometimes life makes you
the windshield,
sometimes life makes you
the bug.

Grace under pressure
is arriving for church late
and walking all the way down
to the front row.

~~~

No matter how nice the weather,
the cat'll always have her kittens in the barn.

~~~

The best place to live
is a hotbed of tranquility.

~~~

If you don't stand for something,
you're likely to fall for anything.

Get up early,
even if you don't have nothing
particular to do.

~~~

Don't pee off the porch
unless it's your porch.

~~~

A good scare is worth more than a ton of advice.

~~~

It doesn't matter how they did it up north.

~~~

If you've got all your eggs in one basket,
watch the basket.

Don't let anyone borrow
your work gloves.

Go barefoot when you can.

Ounce for ounce,
the meanest critter
in the world is a red bug.

Always carry a pocketknife.

~~~

A convenience store ain't
if it won't cash your paycheck.

Pay your child support on time.

~~~

When you move to a new place,
stop by your neighbors' at least once
to let them get a good look at you.

~~~

Don't dress up.

~~~

Don't wear out your welcome.

~~~

Leave
before they want you to go.

Be sure you say goodbye
to everyone individually, by name.

~~~

If your new neighbors stop by
to help you move in, don't insult them
by offering to pay them for their help.

~~~

Beware of anyone
who seems to have plenty of time
to tell you how to run your business.

~~~

Some people are experts
at giving really lousy advice.

Never tell anyone how to do something
unless you're asked.

~~~

On the other hand, if you ask for advice,
don't argue with it.
If you don't like it,
just say thank you; then ignore it.

~~~

Respect your elders.

~~~

Don't sass your mama.

~~~

Eat your green beans.

Wash up before supper.

~~~

There can never be
too many desserts to choose from.

~~~

Underpin your mobile home.

~~~

Don't miss the school's fall festival.

~~~

Join in the cakewalk.

~~~

Root for the Braves.

~~~

Wear long sleeves when picking blackberries.

If your eyes pooch out on stems,
your underwear is too tight.

Play your Patsy Cline
albums often.

Loaf.

Hang a tire swing
in the backyard for the kids.

The best way to get rain
is to wash and wax your car.

Take time to sit on the porch swing
and listen to the crickets sing.

Go for ice cream on a hot night.

Catch fireflies
and put them in a jar,
but always let them go
the next morning.

Some groundhogs are destined
to hang on a fence.

~~~

Never forget what your mama taught you.

~~~

Never turn down a home-cooked meal.

~~~

Pay attention to your blessings.

~~~

All kids really need is a box to play with.

~~~

Make mud pies.

~~~

Never forget what you owe.

Don't take anything or anybody
for granted.

~~~

Be polite, even if it ain't stylish.

~~~

Never get too old to play.

~~~

You have to go to a tractor pull at least once.

~~~

Put up with family.

~~~

Be mindful of the example you're setting.

Be patient and smile a lot.

~~~

Babies are nice people.

~~~

Sip honeysuckle.

~~~

If the coast is clear, just peel off your clothes
and go skinny dipping.

~~~

Go on a hayride.

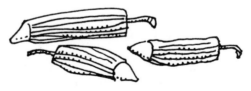

OKRA — THe PoD of the GoDs

Spanish Moss

Creeks are for wading through,
trees are for climbing,
and fences are for sitting on.

Help somebody out—
it'll make you feel better.

A lady never "carries on."

Poor is when you ain't got what you want,
but po' is when you ain't got nothing.

Nobody ever starved on beans and corn bread.

~~~

Better to sleep in the shed
than in a cozy bed with a nagging woman.

Let
sleeping dogs
lie.

Slow down.

~~~

Never ask someone to do
what you wouldn't do yourself.

The early bird
gets to the yard sale before it's even set up.

Reminisce.

Wear a straw hat
when working
in the garden.

Pay attention to your kids
or they'll grow right past you.

~~~

Make your own fun.

~~~

A man ain't ever comfortable in a three-piece suit.

Some folks
can raise a bigger stink
than a polecat
under a porch.

If you pass gas, don't blame it on the dog.

Age gracefully.

~~~

Cheaters never prosper.

~~~

Better to pass gas and bear the shame,
than not pass gas and bear the pain.

There's always room for one more at the table.

~~~

Never give folks a reason to doubt you.

~~~

There's plenty of satisfaction
in a job done right.

~~~

Tomatoes and saltines are made for each other.

~~~

A cool head and a warm heart keep a body
at a steady temperature.

Just because
a man
sticks his head
under the hood
doesn't mean
he knows
how to fix the car.

Not all asses walk on four legs.

~~~

It's smarter to plow around a stump
than through it.

Never make fun
of someone else's
pickup truck.

**Never make fun
of someone else's
hat.**

Make sure there are no witnesses around
when telling a fishing story.

~~~

True gun control
is hitting what you aim at.

If you ain't the one
making dust,
you're liable to be eating it.

If it was good enough
for Grandaddy,
it's good enough for you.

Stop signs are
for target practice.

You never get used
to the humidity.

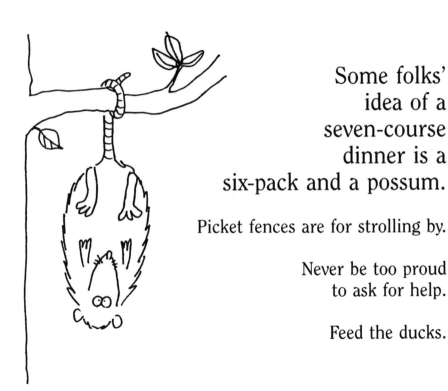

Some folks'
idea of a
seven-course
dinner is a
six-pack and a possum.

Picket fences are for strolling by.

Never be too proud
to ask for help.

Feed the ducks.

Don't think you're immortal.

~~~

Go to the drive-in while it's still there.

~~~

Things happen faster than they used to.

~~~

A woman should learn to stomp her foot
if she wants to get her way.

~~~

A tad of powder, a little paint,
makes a woman what she ain't.

~~~

The finest home security system in the world
is a loud dog and a handy shotgun.

Sometimes the best BBQ
comes out of a
fifty-gallon barrel.

As long as the sun's shining,
things never seem quite so bad.

Right is right and don't wrong nobody.

~~~

If you do the shellin',
someone else should do the shuckin'.

Pecans

If you want to be seen, stand up.

~~~

If you want to be heard, speak up.

~~~

If you want to be appreciated, shut up.

Your sleeve ain't no handkerchief.

~~~

Know when it's time to put your tools
back in the truck and head home.

~~~

Don't fret over the mouse
in your kitchen
when the hogs
are in the garden.

~~~

The most-read book in the house
can always be found
in the bathroom.

Some politicians are so slippery,
they have to wear suspenders
to keep their pants up.

~~~

A woman is as young as she feels
like telling you she is.

~~~

A mess of crappie is real good eating.

~~~

A true gentleman is a gentleman always.

~~~

Kinfolk will always take you in if you're in trouble.
However, some folks prefer the trouble to the kin.

The best landscape border for the patio
is your old tires.

Good manners
make life
more pleasant
for everyone.

Chew
with your mouth
closed.

Don't sing at the table.

It's okay to mix your corn bread and beans,
but not your peas and potatoes.

Let the kids go through the serving line first.

~~~

Put their table as far as possible
from the adults' table.

Don't clip
your nails
in church.

Practice modesty
in all situations—
especially when
you've got reason
to brag.

Nobody
likes someone
who's uppity,
even when he has
a right to be.

If you're about to drop off during the sermon,
pretend to study your Bible.

Drive extra careful on any road
that has grass growing down the middle of it.

~~~

The best time to practice humility
is when the policeman
pulls you over.

~~~

A country store is for swappin' stories at.

~~~

The louder the cackle,
the bigger the egg.

~~~

Don't air your dirty linens for the neighbors to see.

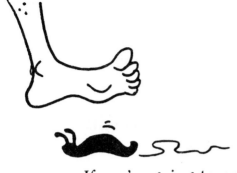

Never step on a slug
barefoot.

Eat what you can,
can what you can't.

If you're going to preach at someone,
pause on occasion
to see if you've got any "amens."

~~~

Always take the time to share what's on your heart.

~~~

Sing harmony whenever possible.

Everyone eventually returns home,
even if it's in a box.

~~~

If you're really determined to do something,
go at it whole hog.

~~~

Folks don't live longer in the South —
it just seems that way.